THE CHOICE CARNIVAL

The Choice Carnival

A STORY ABOUT CHOICES, MISTAKES, AND HOW MINDS REALLY WORK

ZACHARY URBAN

Book One of
Professor Ponder's Academy of Magnificent Mistakes

First Edition, 2025

Professor Ponder's Academy of Magnificent Mistakes

Book One: The Choice Carnival

www.zacharyurban.com

For Isabella and Isaiah — may your choices always be your own.

A Note from the Author

A few years ago, I started noticing something about my two children.

My daughter, the older of the two, is a careful saver and a serious student. She'll sit with a decision for days. She rarely takes a chance she hasn't already mapped out three steps ahead. My son is the opposite—he loves games, he loves wagers, and he experiences the moment of taking a risk as something like delight. They are siblings raised in the same house by the same parents, and they approach the world from completely different starting points.

Watching them, I kept noticing that each of them was running into the same kind of trouble—just from opposite directions. My daughter was missing opportunities because she was afraid to lose. My son was making impulsive bets because he wasn't pausing to ask what the odds actually were. They were both making decisions without understanding what was driving the decision, and they were both, in different ways, paying for it.

I'd been reading about behavioral economics—the study of how human beings actually make choices, as opposed to how we'd make them if we were perfectly rational. It struck me that the field's central insights would be more useful to my children at age ten than they had been to me at thirty. So I wrote this book for them, and for any kid trying to figure out the world.

The Choice Carnival is a story, first and always. The twins Lila and Leo are loosely based on my children, and they go on a real adventure through a magical carnival. But hidden inside the adventure is a curriculum: nine of the most powerful concepts in behavioral economics, taught the way I think they should be taught—through experience, with humor, in a voice that respects the reader.

My hope is that young readers come away with two things: a fun story they want to read again, and a small toolkit of questions they can use for the rest of their lives. *What's my anchor? Is this still worth it? Am I really choosing, or am I just following?* These are questions the most thoughtful adults I know ask themselves daily. There's no reason kids can't start asking them now.

If this book helps even one child make one better decision—a small one, an ordinary one—then it has done its work.

Zachary Urban

Wheat Ridge, Colorado

What You'll Learn

This book is a story about twins at a magical carnival—but hidden inside it are nine real ideas from behavioral economics. Here's what each chapter teaches:

Anchoring: The first number we hear pulls our thinking—even when it's wrong.

Delayed Gratification: Waiting for a bigger reward instead of taking a small one now.

Framing: How something is described changes how we feel about it.

Loss Aversion: We fear losing things more than we enjoy gaining things.

Herd Mentality: Following the crowd without thinking for ourselves.

Paradox of Choice: Too many options can make it harder to decide.

Sunk Cost Fallacy: Don't keep going just because you've already started.

Reciprocity: Feeling we must give back when we receive something.

Probability: Understanding chances to make smarter decisions.

For additional lesson plans, teacher guides or to listen to the Choice Carnival Playlist visit www.ZacharyUrban.com

Contents

Chapter One

The Choice Carnival Opens

The Wheel of Wants

Ashwood Bluff was the kind of town where nothing exciting ever happened. The biggest news all year was Mrs. Higginbottom's grumpy cat, Whiskers, getting stuck in the same twisty oak tree—again. The fire truck came and everything. Everyone gathered on the sidewalk to watch, and Whiskers glared down at them like she'd done it on purpose just to ruin their afternoon.

But once a year, something downright magical crashed into town like a runaway rollercoaster: Professor Ponder's Choice Carnival.

It arrived in the dead of night. One moment the old fairgrounds at the edge of town sat empty, just weeds and a rusty fence. Then morning came, and suddenly the sky above it blazed with color. Twelve-year-old twins Lila and Leo smelled it before they even opened their eyes—caramel apples and cotton candy so thick and sweet it floated right through their bedroom windows like a delicious fog.

Lila shot out of bed like a cannonball. "It's HERE!" she hollered, her wild curls bouncing in every direction. She was already pulling on her sneakers before Leo had even found his glasses.

Leo sat up slowly, squinting. He was the kind of kid who liked to think before he moved. Where Lila was a firecracker—bright and loud and always going off at the wrong moment—Leo was more like a magnifying glass, carefully studying things before he touched them. He found his glasses on the nightstand, settled them on his nose, and peered out the window at the colorful towers rising over the treetops.

"Huh," he said.

"HUH?" Lila appeared in the doorway, one shoe on and one hand on her hip. "That's all you've got? It's the Choice Carnival, Leo! Let's GO!"

They ran the whole six blocks, Lila pulling ahead the entire way while Leo jogged steadily behind. When they skidded to a stop at the entrance, both of them went quiet for a moment.

The fairgrounds had transformed completely. Rides spun and soared like dizzy dragons against the bright blue sky. Game booths clinked and clanged with the promise of prizes—stuffed animals as big as refrigerators, glittery trophies, shiny gadgets that caught the light and threw it everywhere. The air smelled so good it made your stomach growl even if you'd just had breakfast. Somewhere a calliope played a tune that made your feet want to dance whether you liked it or not.

At the entrance, a giant sign glowed with golden letters that actually seemed to wiggle, like they were alive and excited to be there: *Welcome to Professor Ponder's Choice Carnival! Earn Your Decision-Maker Badge—If You Dare!*

"A badge?" Lila said, her grin spreading so wide it nearly reached her ears. "That's *mine*. I bet it's sparkly. I bet it helps you pick the best stuff."

"Sounds like a trick," Leo muttered, pushing his glasses up his nose and studying the sign. "Carnivals always want something from you. This is probably just a fancy way to make us spend all our allowance."

"You think everything is a trick."

"Everything usually *is* a trick."

"You're such a worrywart." Lila grabbed his arm and yanked him through the golden archway before he could say another word. They tumbled into a world buzzing with wonders.

For a few seconds, even Leo forgot to be suspicious. Everywhere he looked, something amazing was happening. A girl on a high-wire juggled flaming torches. A boy somewhere behind them laughed so hard at a game that he fell down. The smells layered on top of each other—popcorn, cinnamon, something chocolatey and warm—and the sounds wove together into one great cheerful roar.

Then a voice cut through it all like a foghorn wearing a tuxedo.

"Welcome, welcome, WELCOME!"

The twins turned. Standing smack in the middle of the midway, as if he'd been there all along and they just hadn't noticed, was the most extraordinary person either of them had ever seen. He was tall—very tall—and dressed in a purple suit that sparkled like a clear night sky full of stars. His top hat was so tall it seemed dangerous, wobbling slightly as if it had its own opinions about which direction to lean. And his smile—his smile was enormous. The kind of smile that made you feel like he'd been waiting specifically for *you*.

"I'm Professor Ponder!" the man boomed, sweeping his hat off in a bow that somehow didn't upset it at all. "And you, my marvelous, magnificent twins, are about to begin the greatest adventure of your summer—the hunt for the Decision-Maker Badge!"

Lila's hand shot into the air. "What do we have to do?"

Professor Ponder's eyes twinkled. "Simple! Explore my midway, face its challenges, and prove you can make smart choices. Every decision you make here matters more than you might think."

Leo frowned. "What does that mean? Like, if I pick the wrong popcorn flavor, I lose?"

"Oh, it's much more interesting than popcorn," Professor Ponder said. "Let's start easy. Step right up to the Wheel of Wants!"

He swept his arm toward a giant spinning wheel nearby, painted in every color of the rainbow. Each section held a different prize: "Free Popcorn," "Double Tickets," "Giant Stuffed Bear," "Skip the Line," "Mystery Prize." A small crowd had gathered around it, watching a carnival worker spin it for each person who stepped up.

Lila didn't hesitate. She bounded forward and grabbed the handle with both hands. "Okay, wheel! Give me something GOOD!" She gave it a mighty spin. It whirred like a tiny tornado, the colors blurring together, then slowed—click, click, click—and landed on: **Double Tickets**.

"YES!" Lila pumped her fist as the Professor handed her two shiny golden tickets. "Two whole tickets! That's twice as many things I can do!"

Leo stepped up next, more carefully, as if a thoughtful spin might produce better results. He sent the wheel turning at a steady pace. It clicked to a stop on: **Skip the Line**.

The worker handed him a laminated pass with a star on it. Leo turned it over in his hands. "Wait," he said slowly. "You got two tickets—that's two chances at two different games or rides. I just got... permission to not wait?"

"The prizes aren't even close to the same," Lila said, holding her tickets up to the light triumphantly. "Mine are *obviously* better. I get more stuff."

Leo wasn't so sure, but he tucked his pass in his pocket. "We'll see."

Professor Ponder beamed at them both. "Smart observations already! Your choices have set you on two very different paths. The badge awaits those who can figure out which prize is *truly* worth more—and that might not be as obvious as it seems."

Lila clutched her tickets and looked out across the glittering midway, already calculating which game to try first. Leo kept his hand in his pocket, fingers wrapped around the laminated pass.

One thing was already clear: this wasn't just any carnival. And that badge wasn't going to be easy to earn.

Chapter Two

The Anchoring Arcade

Anchoring

The next morning, Lila was ready to go before the sun had fully decided to show up. She'd spent half the night lying awake making plans. Two tickets meant two chances at two games. She'd already decided on the Ring Toss—everyone knew the prizes there were the best, huge stuffed animals stacked to the ceiling—and the Balloon Darts for something she could actually carry home.

Leo had spent the night thinking too, but he'd been thinking about the pass. *Skip the Line.* At first it seemed like the obvious loser—Lila had *two* whole tickets, and he got a piece of laminated cardboard. But the more he thought about it, the more interesting it seemed.

They arrived at the fairgrounds just as the carnival was coming to life for the day, workers rolling up canvas doors and turning on lights. Lila made a beeline for the Ring Toss.

The line was enormous.

It stretched halfway around the game booth, kids of all ages shuffling forward inch by inch while a bored-looking carnival worker waited at the front. Lila stared at it. "It's fine," she said. "It'll move fast."

It didn't move fast.

Twenty minutes later, Lila was still three kids from the front, and she'd run out of things to look at. Leo, meanwhile, had spotted the sign—SKIP THE LINE PASS ACCEPTED—walked right to the front, and tossed his three rings in about forty-five seconds. He won a small rubber bouncy ball. It wasn't a giant stuffed animal. But as he strolled back past Lila, she noticed that he was already playing with it, tossing it idly and catching it, while she was still standing in line with nothing to do but shuffle forward.

"Having fun?" he asked pleasantly.

"Quiet," she said.

When she finally reached the front, she tossed her rings, won nothing, and used her second ticket on the Balloon Darts. She popped two balloons and won a keychain. It was fine. It was very fine. She stared at it for a moment, then looked at Leo's bouncy ball, then looked at how much of the morning they'd spent standing in a line.

"Okay," she said finally. "Maybe your pass was better."

"I didn't say anything."

"You were *thinking* it very loudly."

Professor Ponder appeared out of nowhere—he had an uncanny talent for this—his purple suit bright as a grape lollipop in the morning light. "Good morning, my clever adventurers! How are we feeling about yesterday's choices?"

"Complicated," Lila said.

"Excellent! Complicated is where the learning lives." He spread his arms wide toward a building they hadn't noticed yesterday, its facade covered in blinking lights and flashing bulbs.

A sign above the door sparkled in gold and red: *The Anchoring Arcade: Where Your First Guess Hooks You!*

"Hooks us?" Leo squinted. "That sounds ominous."

"It sounds *fun*," Lila said, and walked in.

The inside of the Anchoring Arcade was one long room full of guessing games. Guess the weight of the watermelon. Guess how many rubber ducks are in the pool. Guess the length of the longest piece of spaghetti (it was a weird carnival). But in the dead center of the room, where everyone's eyes went first, sat a glass jar the size of a small child, absolutely stuffed to the brim with jellybeans in every color imaginable—red and yellow and green and purple and orange, piled so high they pressed against the glass lid.

A carnival worker in a striped vest stood beside it, holding a clipboard. "Step right up! Guess how many jellybeans and win a prize! Plus—" she dropped her voice to a stage whisper that carried across the whole room, "—a step closer to that badge."

A crowd had gathered. Lila and Leo pushed to the front just as a boy with very loud sneakers elbowed past them and shouted at the jar: "FIVE HUNDRED! I bet it's five hundred jellybeans!"

His friends all nodded like this was a brilliant assessment.

Lila studied the jar. Five hundred. She tilted her head left, then right. It did look like... a lot... of jellybeans... maybe around... "Yeah," she said, picking up a slip of paper from the stack and scribbling her guess. "Five-twenty-five. That seems right."

Leo had been quiet, doing something methodical. He'd picked a small section of the jar—maybe twenty jellybeans across, four or five deep—and was counting quietly under his breath. Then he looked at the whole jar and counted how many of those sections could fit. It took him longer than Lila. He wrote down 1,250.

"Time's up!" the worker called, collecting slips. She made a show of counting, double-checking, looking at her own records. Then she turned to the crowd. "The real number of jellybeans in this jar... is one thousand, two hundred!"

A gasp went through the crowd. A few kids groaned. The boy with the loud sneakers looked betrayed by mathematics.

Leo's jaw dropped. "I was fifty off!"

Lila stared at her slip. 525. "Mine's... less than half the real number," she said slowly. "That's not even close."

"What happened?" Leo asked, turning to look at her.

"That loud kid," Lila said. "He shouted five hundred, and my brain just... grabbed onto it. It was like his number pulled my guess down toward it, even though I hadn't really counted anything. I just thought, 'Yeah, five hundred-ish sounds about right.'"

Leo nodded slowly. "It gave you a starting point. A bad one. And once you had a starting point, you adjusted a little bit from there instead of thinking it through fresh."

"So his wrong number made my guess wrong too."

"Exactly!"

Professor Ponder materialized between them, producing a single jellybean seemingly from thin air and twirling it between his fingers. "Aha! You've just stumbled onto one of the sneakiest tricks in all of human thinking. It's called **anchoring**."

"Anchoring," Lila repeated.

"When the first piece of information we hear—that *anchor*—drags our judgment toward it, even when that first number has nothing to do with the real answer," Professor Ponder explained. "Lila, your brain latched onto five hundred and never really let go. Leo, you ignored the shout and calculated your own starting point instead."

Leo smirked slightly, trying to be modest about it and failing.

"This doesn't just happen at carnival games," Professor Ponder continued. "It happens in stores all the time. If you see a jacket marked 'Originally $200, Now $80,' your brain thinks, *Great deal!* But what if the jacket was never really worth two hundred dollars? What if eighty dollars is actually too much? The anchor—that original price—has already shaped how you feel."

"So any first number I see is trying to hook me," Leo said.

"Precisely! For the badge, the question to always ask yourself is: *What's my anchor?* And then: *Is this anchor trustworthy, or should I ignore it and think fresh?*"

The worker handed Leo a small glowing bouncy ball as his prize. He held it up and it caught the light, throwing little sparkles across the ceiling.

Lila crossed her arms, not pouting—she was absolutely not pouting—and looked back at the jellybean jar. "Can I try again?"

"You certainly may," the worker said.

Lila stared at the jar for a long moment. This time she covered her ears so she couldn't hear anyone else's guesses. She counted a section, estimated the whole, and wrote down 1,180.

Close enough for second prize: a small, slightly deflated stuffed bear.

She carried it under her arm as they headed back out into the midway. In the distance, above a towering hedge maze, she could already smell something warm and sweet drifting on the breeze. A sign poked up above the green walls: *The Marshmallow Maze: Patience Pays Off!*

"Marshmallows," Lila breathed, her eyes lighting up like the arcade sign. "That's next."

"Let's see if you can wait for them this time," Leo said.

Lila thought about the Ring Toss line, and the keychain, and the slightly deflated bear. "I'm a changed person," she announced. "I am completely patient now."

Leo looked at how fast she was already walking toward the maze. He decided not to comment.

Anchoring: *The first number or piece of information we hear can pull our thinking toward it—even when that first number is totally wrong. Always ask: What's my anchor?*

Chapter Three

The Marshmallow Maze

Delayed Gratification

The Marshmallow Maze smelled like the inside of a cloud, if clouds were made of pure sugar. As Lila and Leo got closer, the scent got stronger—warm vanilla, toasted sweetness, something caramelized at the edges—until Lila was practically floating toward the entrance on the smell alone.

"I'm a completely patient person," she reminded Leo, mostly reminding herself.

"You said that already."

"I know. I'm reinforcing it."

The maze itself was impressive—hedges twice as tall as Leo, dark green and perfectly trimmed, stretching in every direction like a little city of plants. From outside you couldn't see a single path through. From inside, Lila figured, you probably couldn't see much of anything.

At the entrance stood a carnival worker with a grin so wide it looked almost architectural, like her whole face was built around it. She held a tray covered in a white cloth, and from beneath the cloth came the most persuasive smell Lila had ever encountered.

"Welcome, badge-hunters!" the worker said. "Here's the deal. I can give you one marshmallow right now." She lifted the edge of the cloth to reveal a single perfectly puffy white marshmallow, soft and round as a little moon. "Or—" she paused dramatically, "—you can make it through to the center of the maze, where three marshmallows three times this size are waiting for you. Big as your fist, each of them." She paused again. "But the maze is full of temptations. And there's no skipping ahead."

Lila's hand was already reaching for the single marshmallow before the worker had finished her first sentence.

"One now," she said. "Easy."

She popped it in her mouth. It was extraordinary. Soft and sweet and slightly toasted-tasting somehow, even though it wasn't toasted. She closed her eyes for a second.

"Worth it," she decided.

Leo watched this with his arms folded. "Three," he said. "I'm waiting for three."

"Smart boy," the worker said, and waved them into the maze.

The hedges closed around them immediately. The path turned left, then right, then split into two directions that both looked identical. Lila took the left one at random and Leo followed, his puzzle-solving brain already mapping the turns they'd taken.

Around the first corner, they found a folding table covered in a cloth, and on the cloth sat a display of marshmallows in every color Lila had ever imagined: pink and blue and sunshine yellow and deep purple, all different sizes, all equally fluffy. A little sign read: *Take One! No One's Watching!*

Lila stopped dead.

Her hand moved toward a pink one almost without her permission.

"Hold it," Leo said. He grabbed her wrist. Not hard—just enough to interrupt the motion. "If you eat that one, you're still only getting one marshmallow total. What happened to being patient?"

Lila stared at the pink marshmallow. The pink marshmallow seemed to stare back.

"But they're just sitting there," she said.

"So is the giant prize at the center."

She groaned like she was being asked to climb a mountain. But she pulled her hand back. "Fine. *Fine*. I'm walking away." She walked away very deliberately, and only looked back twice.

The maze got harder. The paths grew narrower and doubled back on themselves. They hit three dead ends in a row. At one point they passed the same unusually-shaped bush twice and Leo made Lila stop so he could look at it from different angles and figure out if they were going in circles. (They were. He solved it by always turning right.)

At one junction they found another temptation: a small table with cups of hot chocolate and mini-marshmallows floating on top. A sign read: *Just a sip! You've earned it!*

"It's not even marshmallows technically," Lila said, eyeing the cups.

"It's a trap," Leo said.

"What if I'm just cold?"

"It's seventy-two degrees."

"What if I'm emotionally cold?"

"Walk, Lila."

She walked.

Further into the maze, they could hear the sounds of other kids—laughter and the occasional triumphant shout—and at one point they passed an opening in the hedge that let them see into a parallel path, where a group of kids were munching happily on handfuls of treats they'd snagged from every table along the way.

Lila stopped and watched them. They did look like they were having a great time.

"They got to eat stuff this whole time," she said. "And we've got nothing."

"We've got the possibility of three giant marshmallows," Leo said.

"Possibility. *Possibility*. They have *actual* food right now."

"They also don't have a shot at the badge."

That settled it. Lila turned away from the happy snacking kids and marched forward with new determination.

The center of the maze, when they finally found it, was worth every second of the wait. It was a small circular clearing with a golden pedestal in the middle, and on the pedestal sat three marshmallows each the size of a small apple—white and perfect and glowing slightly in a beam of sunlight that seemed to hit them at exactly the right angle.

"Oh," Lila said. Just: oh. A sound of pure reverence.

The worker who'd been at the entrance was somehow already there, smiling her enormous smile. "You made it! Both of you. Some badge-hunters turn back before this point." She lifted the marshmallows off the pedestal and handed three to Lila and three to Leo.

Lila bit into hers.

She sat down right there on the grass of the maze center and ate it slowly, because she'd waited this long and she was going to appreciate every bite.

"Okay," she said at last, cheeks full. "*Okay*. That was worth it. That was so, so, so worth it."

Professor Ponder appeared from behind a hedge—he was always appearing from somewhere unexpected, which Lila was beginning to suspect was one of his actual skills—and clasped his hands together with delight.

"Well done, my patient champions! You've just experienced firsthand the power of **delayed gratification**!"

Leo looked up from his own marshmallow. "Waiting for a bigger reward instead of taking the small one right now."

"Precisely! Our brains are wired to want things immediately—it's called present bias, and it's perfectly natural. But the ability to wait, to resist the immediate temptation when something better is coming—that's a superpower. It's how people save money for things they really want. It's how athletes practice for years before a championship. It's how anything big and good in life gets built."

Lila licked sugar off her thumb. "Like, if I saved my allowance instead of buying a tiny thing every week, eventually I could get that skateboard I've been wanting."

"Exactly like that," Professor Ponder said warmly. "Every week you resist a small purchase is one week closer to the big one."

"I mean, I'm not *promising* I'll do that," Lila clarified.

"You don't have to promise anything," Professor Ponder said. "Just remember to ask: *Is it worth the wait?* Sometimes the answer is yes. Sometimes you really do just want the single marshmallow right now, and that's okay too. The important thing is to actually ask the question instead of just grabbing."

Leo finished his last marshmallow and stood up, brushing off his knees. Beyond the clearing, a path led out to the rest of the midway, and already they could see the shimmer of mirrors in a building ahead, its walls reflecting everything around it in warped, twisted ways.

A sign on the building blinked like a star in neon colors: *The Framing Funhouse: Where Things Aren't What They Seem!*

"More tricks?" Lila asked, licking the last of the sugar from her fingers.

"More lessons," Leo said.

Lila stood up, already feeling better and stickier than she had all day. "Let's go."

Delayed Gratification: *Choosing to wait for a bigger, better reward instead of grabbing something small right now. Patience can pay off—ask: Is it worth the wait?*

Chapter Four

The Framing Funhouse

Framing

The Framing Funhouse looked like it couldn't make up its mind about what it wanted to be. The walls were covered in mirrors of all shapes—tall skinny ones that stretched you into a noodle, short round ones that squished you into a pancake, and wavy ones in between that made you look like you were melting and re-solidifying every few seconds. The building itself was slightly crooked, its roof tilting left while its front door leaned right, as if the whole structure was mid-shrug.

Lila stood in front of one of the outside mirrors and watched herself stretch into someone twelve feet tall. "I look incredible," she said.

"You look like a piece of spaghetti wearing a human face," Leo said.

"Same thing."

A carnival worker in a suit covered in question marks was waiting at the door. Actual question marks—printed on the fabric, iron-on patches of them, a question mark pin on the collar.

Even the hat had a question mark on it. Everything about this person said *Are you sure about that?*

"Welcome, badge-chasers!" the worker said, bouncing on their heels with energy. "Are you ready to see how the same thing can look completely, totally, entirely different—depending on how you look at it?"

"That sounds like a riddle," Leo said.

"It sounds like fun," Lila said. "Same thing. Let's go."

The worker handed them each a pair of glasses with swirly lenses, like the inside of a lollipop. "Pop these on! They won't change what you see, exactly—but they'll help you notice things you might have missed."

Lila put hers on immediately. Leo inspected his first, turned them over, held them up to the light, and then put them on.

They stepped inside.

The funhouse was a long hall of mirrors, but these mirrors were different—each one showed a scene instead of a reflection. Like little frozen windows into other places. And each scene had a sign.

The first set showed a lemonade stand. Two mirrors, same stand, same lemonade in the same pitcher. But the signs were completely different.

The left mirror's sign read: *"SUNSHINE LEMONADE! 90% Bubble-Free!"*

The right mirror's sign read: *"SUNSHINE LEMONADE! 10% Bubbly."*

Lila tilted her head left and right, looking from one to the other. "Wait. That's... the same lemonade?"

"Has to be," Leo said. "Ninety percent bubble-free and ten percent bubbly add up to a hundred percent. It's mathematically the same drink."

"But the first one sounds yummy and refreshing, and the second one sounds like it might fizz up my nose."

"Exactly." Leo took his glasses off, polished them on his shirt, and put them back on, as if cleaner glasses would help him understand faster. "It's the words. Not the drink."

Professor Ponder was already in the funhouse, leaning against one of the mirrors with his arms crossed and a satisfied expression, like a teacher who'd been waiting for exactly this moment.

"You've found it!" he said. "You've spotted **framing**. The way information is presented—the frame around it, so to speak—changes how we feel about it, even when the underlying facts are identical."

Lila pulled off her swirly glasses and stared at them. "So these glasses weren't actually doing anything special?"

"Not at all," Professor Ponder said cheerfully. "Props! For atmosphere. The real glasses you need are in here." He tapped his temple.

"What else is framed in here?" Leo asked, already moving deeper into the funhouse.

The next set of mirrors showed a plate of vegetables. Left sign: *"Eat Your Broccoli—It's Good For You!"* Right sign: *"Only 3 out of 10 kids eat enough vegetables. Are you one of them?"*

Lila stared at both. "The second one makes me weirdly want to eat broccoli, because now it's like a competition."

"Versus the first one making you want to argue with your parents," Leo said.

"Right. But it's still just broccoli."

Further along, a mirror pair showed a coin toss. Left sign: *"You have a 70% chance of winning!"* Right sign: *"You have a 30% chance of losing!"*

Leo stood perfectly still in front of these for a while.

"They're the same bet," he said finally.

"But the first one feels exciting and the second one feels scary," Lila said.

"Exactly the same bet. Exactly the same odds. The framing just makes one feel like an opportunity and one feel like a risk."

Professor Ponder appeared between them. "You're getting it! And this happens everywhere. When a doctor says 'ninety percent of patients recover,' that feels very different than 'ten percent of patients don't recover'—even though it's the same information. When a store says 'four out of five dentists recommend,' it feels authoritative, but what about the fifth dentist? When your parents say you have 'one hour of screen time left' versus 'only one hour of screen time,' the word *only* frames it as not enough, even if an hour is actually plenty."

"So any time someone's telling me something," Leo said slowly, "I should ask what the *other* way of saying it would be."

"Precisely! For the badge, the question is: *What's the real deal?* Strip away the exciting words or the scary words and ask: what is this actually saying? Look for the plain fact underneath the frame."

Lila thought about this as they moved toward the end of the funhouse, where a small lemonade booth waited—apparently they'd wound through a loop and were back near the front.

"So which lemonade do I actually want?" Lila said, looking at both signs again.

"Well, do you want a drink that's mostly not bubbly, or do you want a drink that's a little bubbly?" Leo said. "Both of those descriptions are exactly true. Pick based on what you actually prefer, not based on which sign sounds better."

Lila considered. "I don't actually mind bubbles," she admitted. "I just didn't want a *fizz disaster*, which is what the second sign made me imagine."

"So the first sign manipulated you into thinking it was better, even though it might actually be the same drink you'd enjoy."

"Okay, I don't love the word *manipulated*, but yes."

She bought a lemonade from the booth. It was, in her opinion, a perfectly good amount of bubbly. Not a disaster at all.

As they walked back out into the full brightness of the midway, a new challenge loomed ahead. The path between two hedge rows led to a larger maze, and a sign cast in flickering green light said: *The Loss Aversion Labyrinth: Where Every Choice Comes with a Risk!*

"Risky stuff," Lila said, finishing her lemonade.

"I'm beginning to think everything here is risky," Leo replied. "That might be the point."

"Then let's figure out what we're actually risking," Lila said, "instead of just how it's framed."

Leo looked at her with something that might have been impressed. "Look at you, applying the lessons."

Lila grinned. "Don't make it weird. Let's go."

Framing: *The way information is presented changes how we feel about it, even when the underlying facts are exactly the same. Ask: What's the real deal?*

Chapter Five

The Loss Aversion Labyrinth

Loss Aversion

The Loss Aversion Labyrinth was bigger than the Marshmallow Maze—much bigger, with hedges twice as tall and paths that twisted in ways that seemed almost deliberately confusing. From outside the entrance, Lila and Leo could hear other kids somewhere deep inside, and it was impossible to tell whether the sounds were excitement or frustration. Probably both.

A glowing green sign hung above the entrance: *The Loss Aversion Labyrinth: Where Every Choice Comes with a Risk!*

"Risk," Lila said, bouncing on her toes. "I'm good at risk. I embrace risk. Risk and I are friends."

"You fell off the monkey bars last week," Leo said.

"That was a calculated risk that didn't pan out. Totally different."

Professor Ponder was at the entrance, as he seemed to always be—like he somehow knew exactly where they were going next and simply arrived there first.

"Welcome, my daring duo!" he said. "This labyrinth explores one of the most powerful forces in human decision-making: **loss aversion**. The peculiar fact that we hate losing something much, much more than we enjoy gaining the same thing."

Lila frowned. "What do you mean? Losing and gaining are opposites. Shouldn't they feel about the same?"

"That's what you'd think! But research shows that losing something feels about twice as bad as gaining the equivalent thing feels good. If you lose five dollars, the bad feeling is about as strong as the good feeling you'd get from *finding* ten dollars."

"That doesn't seem fair," Lila said.

"It isn't," Professor Ponder agreed pleasantly. "But it's true. And it leads us to make some very strange choices to avoid loss—sometimes choices that cost us more than the thing we were trying to protect."

A carnival worker appeared with two shiny silver keys on a little velvet pillow, offering one to each twin. They were small and old-fashioned looking, with elaborately cut teeth.

"Here are the rules," the worker said. "You each start with a key. The object is to reach the treasure at the center of the labyrinth—and to get there, you'll need a golden key. Along the way, you'll find locked chests. You can trade your current key for a chance at a better one—but some chests are empty, and if you trade for nothing, your key is gone."

"What if we don't trade at all?" Leo asked.

"Then you keep your silver key. But the treasure chest at the center only opens with gold."

Lila weighed her silver key in her palm. It caught the light nicely. It felt satisfying to hold. She hadn't done anything to earn it—it was just given to her—but already she didn't want to lose it.

"Let's go," she said.

The labyrinth was dim and green, the hedges blocking most of the sunlight. The path branched almost immediately. Leo turned right based on some system he'd worked out in the Marshmallow Maze; Lila followed, mostly because she hadn't developed her own system yet.

Around the first corner they found the first chest: small, silver, sitting on a stone pedestal with a sign reading *TRADE YOUR KEY FOR A CHANCE AT MORE—50% ODDS OF UPGRADE!*

"Fifty-fifty," Leo said. "So we might get a better key or we might get nothing."

Lila gripped her key tightly. "What if we get nothing?"

"Then we're worse off. But if we get better, we're closer to the gold."

"I just got this key. I don't want to lose it already."

"Do you want the treasure?"

Lila looked at her key. Looked at the chest. Looked at her key again.

"Fine," she said. "Let's do it."

They traded. She held her breath. The worker who'd materialized from somewhere opened the chest.

Empty.

"UGH." Lila's groan echoed off the hedges. "Told you! Now we've got *nothing*! That key is *gone*!"

"The worker gave us backup keys," Leo said, holding up a second silver key the worker had pressed into his hand. "And look—the sign said fifty percent. We knew this could happen."

"Knowing it could happen and having it actually happen are completely different things," Lila said darkly.

But she took the backup key and moved on.

At the next junction, Leo found a chest first: *TRADE YOUR KEY—70% ODDS OF UPGRADE!*

Seventy percent. Better odds this time.

Leo examined the chest. He thought about the probability lesson they hadn't had yet but somehow already half-knew from just being here. Seventy percent was better than not-seventy percent.

"I'll trade," he said.

He dropped his key in the slot. The worker opened the chest.

A golden key sat inside, gleaming warm yellow in the green dimness of the labyrinth.

"YES," Leo said, in the quiet way he expressed things—a single word with tremendous feeling behind it.

Lila watched him pick it up. She looked at her own silver key. She knew, logically, that his key was better. She knew she should be happy for him. She was... mostly happy for him.

But the feeling of having traded her first key and gotten nothing was still sitting in her chest like a stone. It made her grip her current silver key harder.

"There's another chest ahead," Leo said.

"I'm keeping mine," Lila said immediately. She hadn't consciously decided this. It just came out.

"The odds might be good."

"I already lost one. I'm not losing this one."

Leo paused. He knew better than to push Lila when she had that particular look—jaw set, eyes slightly narrowed, the expression she wore when she'd decided something in her bones. He moved on.

They found two more trading chests on the way to the center. Leo traded once more and got nothing, ending up with his gold key still in hand from the second chest. Lila passed both of them without stopping, clutching her silver key.

At the center of the labyrinth was the treasure chest—large, ornate, trimmed in actual gold paint. Two keyholes: one silver, one gold.

Leo's golden key fit perfectly. He turned it and the chest swung open to reveal two sparkly badges, a stack of midway tickets, and a small trophy with a star on top. He lifted out a badge and tossed it to Lila.

She caught it. Then looked at her silver key. Then at the silver keyhole, which she now had no prizes left to use it on.

Professor Ponder was there, naturally. He always was.

"And now you've both felt it," he said gently. "Lila, when did you stop trading?"

"When I lost the first key," she said.

"Even though losing the first key didn't affect your second key at all?"

She opened her mouth to argue, and then stopped.

"That's **loss aversion**," Professor Ponder said. "The pain of losing that first key was so strong that it made you irrationally protective of the second one—even when the smart move might have been to take a calculated risk. Leo lost a trade too, but it didn't change his willingness to try again when the odds were good."

Leo twirled his remaining tickets. "So, like when someone holds onto an old broken-down car because they can't stand the idea of selling it for less than they paid?"

"Exactly. Or when an investor keeps a failing stock because selling it would make the loss feel *real*, when in reality the loss has already happened whether they sell or not." Professor Ponder looked at Lila kindly. "The key question is: *What could I gain?* Not: *What have I already lost?* The first key is gone either way. The only thing you can actually control is what you do next."

Lila pinned the sparkly badge to her shirt and was quiet for a moment.

"I'm going to think about that for a while," she said.

"Good," said Professor Ponder. "That's exactly the right response."

Ahead, they could already hear the cheerful music of something spinning, and a breezy sound of laughter. A bright sign blinked in the distance: *The Herd Carousel: Do You Follow or Lead?*

"More," Lila said, the badge catching the light as she moved. She said it not like a question or a complaint, but like a statement of readiness.

Leo followed. "More."

Loss Aversion: *We feel the pain of losing something about twice as much as we feel the joy of gaining the same thing. Don't let fear of loss stop you—ask: What could I gain?*

Chapter Six

The Herd Carousel

Herd Mentality

The Herd Carousel was impossible to miss. It was enormous—the biggest ride in the midway by a significant margin—painted in red and gold with hand-carved horses that went up and down in stately loops while a pipe organ piped a merry tune that wormed its way into your head and stayed there. Even from a distance it looked grand and old-fashioned and like exactly the kind of ride that belonged in a magical carnival.

It also had the longest line Lila had ever seen at any ride anywhere.

The line started at the ticket booth, wound around the entire carousel once, doubled back, and ended somewhere near a funnel cake stand. There were easily sixty kids in it, shuffling forward in the slow way that lines always move when you really want to get to the front.

Lila and Leo stopped and looked at it.

"Wow," Lila said.

"Yeah," Leo agreed.

A sign above the line read: *The Herd Carousel: Do You Follow or Lead? Longest line of the midway—must be worth it!*

Professor Ponder drifted up beside them, his purple suit vivid against all the red and gold of the carousel. "Ahh," he said, with the tone of someone who has been watching something unfold exactly as expected. "And here we are."

"It's so popular," Lila said. She couldn't help it—seeing sixty kids wanting something made her want it too. The logic felt automatic: *that many people can't be wrong*. "It must be incredible. Like, if everyone's waiting that long, the ride has to be worth it, right?"

"Does it?" Professor Ponder asked mildly.

Lila was already stepping toward the end of the line. The pull was almost physical—like something tugging her sleeve. Everyone's doing it. Get in line. Don't miss out.

Then Leo grabbed her arm.

"Hold on," he said. "Let's actually look at this."

"Look at what? It's a carousel. We can see it from here."

"Look at the people coming *off* it."

They watched. After a few minutes, a group of kids who'd been on the ride shuffled off the exit ramp. They looked... fine. They weren't screaming with joy. They weren't high-fiving each other or rushing back to get in line again. They were mostly just walking away, one of them checking her phone, one of them debating with a friend about where to get food next.

Not one of them looked like someone who had just experienced the ride of their lives.

"Hm," Lila said.

"Also," Leo added, "look at the people *in* the line."

The line was long—sixty people—but it was also very quiet for sixty people who were supposedly excited about something. A group near the middle were doing homework. Actual homework, with notebooks and pencils. Near the back, two kids were playing a card game they'd brought from home. Nobody in the entire line was talking about the carousel.

"They're not even excited about the ride," Lila said slowly. "They're just... standing there."

"Why'd they get in line?" Leo asked.

Lila thought about it. "Because it was long? Because a long line means it's good?"

A carnival worker in red and gold came over to them, arms spread wide. "Hop on, badge-hunters! This is our most popular attraction! Everyone loves the Herd Carousel!"

"Why is it so popular?" Leo asked.

The worker blinked. That was apparently not a question they'd been asked before. "Well—because everyone's in line for it."

"But why did the first people get in line?"

The worker thought about this for a moment, looking genuinely uncertain. "I... think someone influential got in line early in the day and other people followed?"

"And then other people followed those people?" Leo said. "And so on?"

"I suppose so."

Professor Ponder stepped forward, straightening his lapels. "This is what we call **herd mentality**, my friends! The tendency to look at what everyone else is doing and assume it must be the right thing—often without asking *why* they're doing it."

Lila looked at the line. Sixty-something kids, waiting for a mediocre carousel ride, because other people had waited for a mediocre carousel ride, because other people had before that, going all the way back to some original person who maybe hadn't even wanted to ride it that much but saw a sign and thought: *why not?*

"It happens everywhere," Professor Ponder continued. "When a restaurant is full, people assume the food must be good. When a book is a bestseller, people buy it partly because it's a bestseller. When a toy sells out, parents rush to buy it not because they've researched whether it's good, but because the fact that everyone else wants it makes it feel more valuable."

"It's like the anchoring thing," Leo said. "Except instead of a number pulling you, it's people."

"Beautifully put! Information from other people is called a *social cue*, and social cues can be very useful—most of the time, popular things are popular for reasons. But the herd can also be completely wrong. It's gotten a lot of people into a very boring line."

Lila scanned the midway. Away from the carousel, quieter and less crowded, was a dart game she'd barely noticed before. The prizes hanging from the back wall were good ones—big stuffed animals, iridescent trophies, the kind of things you'd actually want. And there was almost no one playing.

"That game looks good," she said.

"Nobody's at it," Leo noted. "So probably most people walked right past it."

"Because they were following the crowd to the carousel."

"Which is mediocre."

"So the better game has no line."

They looked at each other.

"Badge-level choosers," Lila said, with some satisfaction.

They walked to the dart game. The worker there looked pleasantly surprised to have customers.

Lila lined up her first dart, thought about what she actually wanted to aim for instead of just throwing quickly, and launched it. Bullseye. She pumped her fist so hard her whole body shook.

"YES! I'm taking the giant dragon."

"That's not the dragon, that's a lizard."

"It's a *dragon* in my heart, Leo."

Leo played more carefully and won a small prize he was happy with. Behind them, the carousel continued its stately rotations, its long line shuffling slowly forward, kids doing homework and playing cards while they waited.

Professor Ponder watched the twins with evident pride. "The question isn't *what is everyone doing?* The question is *what do I actually want?* Those are two very different questions, and the answers don't always match."

"For the badge," Lila said, clutching her stuffed dragon-lizard, "ask: do I want this, or am I just following?"

"Exactly right."

The midway stretched ahead of them, and not far along it, a tent glittered with twinkling lights. Its sign sparkled with gold and silver: *The Paradox of Choice: Too Many Options, Too Little Time!*

"Paradox," Leo said. "That means contradiction. A thing that seems impossible but is true."

"Great," Lila said. "More impossible truths. I'm starting to feel like this carnival is doing something to my brain."

"Good," said Professor Ponder, from somewhere he wasn't supposed to be yet. "That's the whole point."

Herd Mentality: When we follow what everyone else is doing without thinking about whether we actually want it. Think for yourself—ask: Do I want this, or am I just following? *?*

Chapter Seven

The Paradox of Choice

Paradox of Choice

The tent glittered from the outside, which made sense when you stepped inside and discovered it was almost entirely covered in lights—strands of tiny bulbs running along every seam and edge, cascading down the walls, outlining the tables and prize displays in gold and white. It was beautiful and slightly overwhelming. Lila immediately loved it. Leo immediately started trying to count the light bulbs.

The tent was set up like a prize gallery. All around the walls, wonderful things were displayed on pedestals under small spotlights: a cuddly purple unicorn with a silver horn; a sleek robot that beeped and rolled on little wheels; a pogo stick that had somehow been made to look elegant; a kite shaped like a dragon (Lila elbowed Leo: "See? Dragon."); and in the center, on a slightly elevated pedestal, a mystery box wrapped in gold paper and tied with a bow, giving nothing away.

A carnival worker with a grin that somehow managed to be even wider than the one in the Marshmallow Maze bounced toward them. "Welcome, welcome! Step up, badge-hunters! The deal is simple—pick one prize. Any prize. Just one!"

"That seems easy," Lila said.

"And you've got thirty seconds to decide."

"That seems less easy," Leo said.

"Time starts—" the worker clicked a stopwatch, "—NOW!"

Lila's head swiveled like a lighthouse. Unicorn. Robot. Pogo stick. Dragon kite. Mystery box. Unicorn. Robot. Pogo stick. Dragon kite. Mystery box. Unicorn—

"Oh no," she said.

Her feet carried her toward the unicorn, because it was cuddly and she'd always liked cuddly things. Her hands almost touched it. But then the robot beeped from across the tent, and it was such a satisfying *beep*, exactly the right pitch, and she turned to look at it, and it was very shiny, and shiny things were also excellent—

"The robot might actually be useful," she said to herself. "Or the pogo stick. I haven't bounced on a pogo stick in forever, that could be really fun, or the kite—I could fly the kite at the park—but what if the mystery box has something even better than any of these—"

"Ten seconds," the worker called.

Lila stood in the exact center of the tent with her arms slightly out like she might hug all five prizes simultaneously. She looked at Leo desperately.

Leo was not doing better. He'd picked up the kite, set it down, opened the corner of the mystery box (the worker hadn't said he couldn't), seen nothing visible in the crinkled gold paper, set it down, and was now standing in front of the pogo stick with his arms folded, not bouncing.

The problem was that he could see the merits of each one. The kite was elegant. The robot was functional. The pogo stick was kinetic. The mystery box was *unknown*, which was either the worst or best thing, he genuinely could not decide—

"Five seconds," the worker said cheerfully.

"WHAT DO I DO," Lila said.

"FOUR—"

"WHAT DO I DO, LEO—"

"I DON'T KNOW—"

"THREE—"

"THE UNICORN—"

"TWO—"

"MYSTERY BOX—"

"ONE—"

Lila grabbed the unicorn. Leo grabbed the mystery box. They stood there breathing hard as if they'd run somewhere.

"Time's up!" the worker said, marking something on her clipboard. She handed Lila the unicorn officially and Leo the mystery box. He opened it carefully. Inside: a twisty multicolored puzzle cube, the kind with sixty-seven different moves required to solve it.

Leo's face lit up in a way that almost never happened. "*Oh.* This is perfect."

"Is it?" Lila asked. She was cuddling her unicorn, which was extremely soft, as it turned out. Very correct choice.

"I've wanted one of these for months," Leo said, already turning it in his hands. "I just—didn't know to ask for one."

"That's the mystery box thing, right? You got something good?"

"Something perfect, actually."

Professor Ponder materialized at the entrance of the tent, leaning in the doorway with his hat tilted at a philosophical angle. "How did that feel?" he asked.

"Terrible," Lila said immediately. "Trying to pick was genuinely awful. Like my brain tied itself into a knot."

"Fascinating, isn't it? You both eventually chose well—Lila picked the unicorn because she loves cuddly things, Leo picked the mystery box because he loves puzzles. But the presence of five options made it exponentially harder than if there had only been two."

"Why?" Leo said, not looking up from the cube.

"Because with more options, the cost of each decision gets higher. You can't pick the unicorn without wondering what you might have gotten from the robot. You can't pick the mystery box without the nagging feeling that the kite might have been the right answer. Every option you don't choose becomes a small loss—and remember what we said about loss aversion?"

"We hate losing things twice as much as we enjoy gaining them," Lila said.

"Exactly. So five options doesn't just give you five things to consider—it gives you four potential losses to feel bad about, for whichever one you choose. More options, more potential regret."

"But isn't more choice always better?" Leo asked. "Like, wouldn't it be worse to only have two options?"

"A wonderful question! And the answer is: up to a point. Having *some* choice is better than none—if you could only pick between the unicorn and the robot, that's fine. But research shows that beyond about four or five options, people actually get *less* satisfied with their choices, even if they pick well. Because the what-ifs pile up."

Lila looked at the robot, still sitting on its pedestal, beeping at no one. "I'm a little curious about the robot now," she admitted.

"And you always will be. That's the cost of choice." Professor Ponder stepped fully into the tent. "The trick is to know yourself. Lila, what do you love? Cuddly things. Go immediately to cuddly. Leo, what do you love? Puzzles. Mysteries. Unknowns. Go immediately there. The more clearly you know what you want before the options appear, the less the extra options can confuse you."

"Decide before you get overwhelmed," Leo said.

"Exactly. The question for the badge is: *What do I really want?* Answer it *before* you see all the options if you can—or at the very least, use it to cut through the noise when you're frozen."

Lila was quiet for a moment, stroking her unicorn's silver mane.

"This is a very good unicorn," she said.

"I don't doubt it," Professor Ponder said.

Leo had already solved two sides of his puzzle cube. He held it up to show Lila—two solid colors, a start.

They stepped back out into the midway. The air had shifted slightly, grown a little damper and cooler, and ahead of them the ground seemed to slope downward toward a section of the carnival that had a distinctly murky feel. Tendrils of artificial fog curled along the path. The lights here were dimmer, greenish, like the bottom of a pond.

A sign emerged from the mist, its letters dripping: *The Sunk Cost Swamp: Know When to Walk Away!*

"Swamp," Lila said.

"Yep," Leo said.

They looked at each other. Then walked toward it.

Paradox of Choice: *Having too many options can make us less happy and harder to decide. Know yourself—ask: What do I really want?*

Chapter Eight

The Sunk Cost Swamp

Sunk Cost Fallacy

The approach to the Sunk Cost Swamp smelled like damp earth and mossy things, and the air got thicker the closer you got. Fog machines hummed somewhere out of sight, pumping low white clouds across the ground that curled around their ankles as they walked. The path itself narrowed to a series of flat stones leading into genuine-looking muck—dark brown, slightly glossy, with the occasional bubble popping at the surface.

Lila stopped at the edge and looked down at her shoes. Good shoes. Recently clean, as of this morning. She looked at the muck.

"Is that real?" she asked.

"The bubbles seem real," Leo said.

"The smell seems very real," Lila agreed.

A carnival worker appeared from somewhere—not Professor Ponder this time, a different worker, in waders and a rain slicker that said GUIDE on the back. She was cheerful in the way that people who work outdoors in weather tend to be: genuinely, practically cheerful, unfazed by mud.

"Welcome to the Sunk Cost Swamp!" she said. "Here's the challenge. You start with a pouch of five golden coins." She handed one to each of them—small leather pouches with satisfying weight. Lila opened hers and peeked. Five coins, each stamped with a small star.

"The treasure at the center of the swamp is worth ten coins. But each stone step costs one coin to take—drop it in the slot on the stone, and step forward. You can turn back at any time. When you turn back, you keep whatever coins you have left." The worker paused. "And you can't get the coins back that you've already spent, no matter what."

"No refunds," Leo said.

"No refunds."

"And the treasure at the center—is it definitely there?" Leo asked.

"It's there," the worker confirmed. "Whether it's *worth* going all the way to get it is something only you can decide."

Lila jingled her pouch. She liked the sound. She liked treasure. "I'm doing it," she said immediately. "I'm going to the center. I'm getting that treasure."

"Let's go together," Leo said. "And keep checking whether it's worth continuing."

"That's your version of let's do it?"

"That's my version of let's do it."

The first stone was slippery-looking but held. Lila dropped a coin in the slot—it disappeared with a satisfying *clink*—and stepped forward. The muck on either side was absolutely real, dark and smelly, squelching slightly where the stones pushed into it.

"One coin," Leo said, dropping his own. "Four left."

The path curved. The second stone wobbled slightly underfoot. From somewhere deeper in the swamp came the sounds of other kids—some moving forward, some, from the sound of it, retreating.

Third stone. Three coins left.

This is where things got interesting.

Ahead, Leo could see a group of four kids who'd made it about halfway. They were huddled together looking at their pouches, and even from here you could see they were having a very serious conversation. Then, one by one, they turned around and started back.

"They're quitting," Lila said.

"They're *stopping*," Leo corrected. "Look—they still have coins left. They're going back with something."

Lila watched them slosh back toward the entrance, shoes muddy, expressions a mix of relief and disappointment. "But they were halfway! They came all this way and just gave up?"

"They came halfway and decided the other half wasn't worth the rest of their coins," Leo said. "That's different from giving up."

"Is it?"

Professor Ponder's voice drifted through the fog, not attached to any visible body. It was a little eerie. "Very good question, Lila. Is stopping halfway through the same as giving up?"

"I thought you were a person," Lila said to the fog.

"I am a person," Professor Ponder said, and appeared from behind a particularly convincing fake log. "I just enjoy the atmosphere. Now—the question."

"It feels like giving up," Lila said. "Because we already spent three coins. If we stop now, those three coins are *wasted*."

"Are they?" Leo said. "They're gone whether we stop or keep going. The question is whether spending two more coins to get to the treasure is worth it."

Lila was quiet, which for Lila meant she was thinking hard.

"If we keep going," Leo continued, "we spend two more coins. That's a total of five to cross the whole swamp. The treasure is supposed to be worth ten coins. So mathematically, we come out ahead by five coins."

"But we only have two coins left," Lila said. "And we still need to get back. What if the path back also costs coins?"

The worker, who was standing on a raised platform above the muck, called out: "The path back is free, by the way!"

"Okay, so it's just the forward cost," Leo said. "Two coins left. Two steps left to the center. We break even on coins and get the treasure."

"Which is worth ten coins?"

"Supposedly."

Lila looked forward. She looked at her two remaining coins.

Here was the thing: three coins were already gone. That was done. The fact that she'd spent three coins was completely irrelevant to the question of whether to spend two more—but it felt *incredibly* relevant. It felt like if she stopped now, she'd wasted three coins. Which felt terrible. Which made her want to keep going even if the math didn't quite work.

She recognized this feeling suddenly. It was the same feeling as in the labyrinth when she'd clutched her second key because she'd already lost the first one.

"Oh," she said quietly.

"What?" Leo asked.

"I want to keep going because I don't want the three coins I spent to be a waste. But the three coins are gone no matter what I do. I can't get them back by finishing. I can only decide whether spending two *more* is worth it on its own terms."

Leo looked at her. Then at the path ahead. Then at his two coins.

"So is it?" he asked.

They both thought about this honestly for a moment.

"The treasure is worth ten coins," Lila said. "We'd spend five total to get it. That's a good deal. Let's finish."

"Good logic," Leo said. "But check—what are we getting *instead* of those two coins? We'd have two coins to spend elsewhere in the midway."

Lila thought about the dart game, the arcade, the things they hadn't done yet. Two coins could do something there too.

"I think the treasure is probably worth it," she decided. "Let's go."

They went. The last two stones were the wobbliest, but they made it. The center of the swamp had a small dry island with a chest on it, not ornate like the labyrinth's but solid and wooden and real. Leo lifted the lid.

Inside: a collection of bonus midway tickets, a small golden star badge to add to their collection, and—Lila's personal favorite—a tiny jar of carnival-scented lip balm that smelled like caramel apple.

"This was worth five coins," Lila declared, applying the lip balm immediately.

The path back was indeed free. They squelched their way out, shoes somewhat muddy. Professor Ponder was at the exit, smiling.

"You did something very important in there," he said. "You separated the spent coins—the *sunk cost*—from the question of whether to continue. Most people can't do that. Most people keep going in bad situations because they can't stand to feel like they wasted what they already put in."

"Like watching a terrible movie to the end because you already paid for the ticket," Leo said.

"Exactly. The ticket money is gone either way. The only question is whether spending two more hours of your time on a bad movie is worth it on its own terms—and usually, it isn't. But we finish anyway because we don't want the ticket to feel wasted."

Lila looked down at her shoes. Muddy, but not as bad as she'd feared. "The question for the badge is: is it still worth it. Right now, going forward. Not was it worth it before."

"Perfectly stated," Professor Ponder said.

Above the exit, an arrow pointed toward the next part of the midway, where a rollercoaster was visible through the fog, its tracks looping in spirals against the late-afternoon sky. A sign blazed at its base: *The Reciprocity Rollercoaster: Give a Little, Get a Little!*

"A rollercoaster," Lila said, with the reverence appropriate to the occasion.

"Finally something with no life lessons attached," Leo said.

They were both wrong about that, but they'd find out soon enough.

Sunk Cost Fallacy: *Continuing with something just because you've already invested time or money—even when it's no longer worth it. Ask: Is it still worth it, right now?*

Chapter Nine

The Reciprocity Rollercoaster

Reciprocity

From a distance, the Reciprocity Rollercoaster was spectacular. The tracks wound up into a first drop that looked approximately as tall as a building, corkscrewed twice, did a loop that was somehow sideways, and ended in a section that you couldn't quite see because it was behind a painted wall but that produced screams of a particularly cheerful kind. The whole structure was painted red and silver and caught the afternoon light like something from a dream.

Lila and Leo stood at the base of it and looked up.

"It is very tall," Leo said.

"It's perfectly tall," Lila said. "That's the exact right amount of tall for a rollercoaster."

They'd lost their badges' mud somewhere between the swamp and here, or rather the mud had dried and mostly fallen off during the walk. Their shoes were still somewhat questionable but the rest of them looked presentable. The badges they'd collected clinked softly as Lila adjusted her shirt—the sparkly one from the labyrinth, the gold star from the swamp.

The line for the rollercoaster was reasonable—not the Herd Carousel's sixty-person procession, just a normal fifteen-minute wait that moved steadily. A sign at the entrance to the queue read: *All riders receive a free ticket—Thank You For Riding The Reciprocity Rollercoaster!*

"Free ticket," Lila said. "That's nice of them."

"I wonder why," Leo said.

"Because it's a nice gesture?"

"Maybe," Leo said. "Or maybe there's something attached to it."

"You're suspicious of a free ticket now?"

"I'm just asking the question."

Professor Ponder appeared in line beside them, somehow not having triggered any of the usual reactions from the other kids around them—he was just there, as if he'd always been there, two spots ahead.

"Excellent instincts, Leo," he said quietly. "Keep them."

When they reached the front of the queue, a carnival worker in a red vest handed each of them a shiny golden ticket with the words THANKS FOR RIDING! stamped on it in cheerful letters. "Your complimentary ticket," the worker said warmly. "And may I mention—for just one additional ticket, you can upgrade to our VIP Experience. Priority seating in the front car, a personalized photo taken mid-coaster, and a commemorative magnet!"

Lila looked at her free ticket. Looked at the worker. Felt a very specific feeling that she couldn't quite name—something like *I should do something nice back since they gave me something.*

"I mean," she said. "They gave us a ticket. We could give them a ticket."

"Wait," Leo said. "Would we have wanted the VIP Experience if they hadn't given us a free ticket first?"

Lila thought about it. "Honestly? No. I just want to ride the coaster. I don't need a photo or a magnet."

"So the free ticket is making you feel like you owe them something."

"...Yeah. That's exactly what's happening."

Professor Ponder stepped smoothly beside them as they moved forward in the queue. "What you're feeling is called **reciprocity**. When someone does something for us, we feel a powerful urge to do something back—to balance the scale. It's a deep human instinct, and in many ways it's wonderful. It's the foundation of generosity and cooperation."

"But," Leo said.

"But it can be used on us. Stores give you free samples not just to let you taste the product, but because receiving a gift—even a tiny one—creates a feeling of obligation. That feeling can push you to buy things you wouldn't have bought otherwise."

"So the free ticket isn't really free," Lila said. "It costs us... a feeling."

"Well put. The ticket itself is free. What it costs is the willingness to say 'thank you, but I'll just take the basic experience.'"

Lila looked at the worker, who was smiling in a friendly and entirely genuine-seeming way.

"Do I have to feel bad about keeping the free ticket and not upgrading?" she asked Professor Ponder.

"Not at all! Reciprocity is real and the feeling is real, but you get to decide how to respond to it. The key question is: *Do I actually want this thing?* Not: *Am I obligated to take it because they gave me something?* Generosity given freely doesn't create debt unless you decide it does."

"I don't want the photo and the magnet," Leo said decisively. "I want to ride the coaster and have that be the experience."

"Same," Lila said.

They handed their free tickets to the worker—the worker seemed entirely unbothered, this happened often—and climbed into the second car. Not the front, not the VIP, just two regular seats in a very excellent rollercoaster.

The lap bar came down. The car lurched forward, climbing the first hill with a slow, ratcheting *click click click* that built anticipation the way only a first hill can.

"OKAY," Lila said, gripping the bar. "OKAY. I'm completely fine. This is fine."

"You chose this," Leo reminded her.

"I chose this. This was my free choice. I'm happy about my choice."

"We're at the top."

"I know we're at the—"

They went over.

The drop was perfect—stomach-lifting, breath-stealing, exactly as tall as it had looked from the ground and somehow taller in the experience. Lila screamed with pure joy, which she did not plan, it simply happened. Leo gripped the bar with both hands and grinned, which for Leo was the equivalent of screaming. The corkscrew left them sideways for a half-second that felt like a year. The sideways loop defied several things Leo felt he understood about physics. The hidden section at the end turned out to be a water feature that soaked them both from the waist down.

The car rolled back into the station. Lila sat for a moment with her hair plastered to her face and her eyes wide.

"That," she said, "was worth every free ticket."

"We gave them the free tickets," Leo pointed out, still grinning.

"You know what I mean."

Professor Ponder was waiting at the exit, dry, with two small towels. He handed one to each of them.

"How was it?"

"Perfect," Lila said into her towel.

"And you didn't need the VIP."

"Didn't need anything extra. The ride itself was the thing." She lowered the towel and looked at him. "Reciprocity. Take the free thing, feel grateful for it, but don't let the gratitude push you into buying something you wouldn't have chosen on your own."

"Perfectly stated. The feeling of reciprocity is natural and good—use it to motivate genuine generosity. But recognize when someone is engineering it to sell you something, and ask yourself: *do I really want this?* That question cuts through the feeling every time."

The late-afternoon light was turning golden across the midway. Somewhere ahead, the sounds of the carnival were getting slightly more excited, slightly more charged—like the whole place knew they were coming to the last challenge.

A tent at the far end of the midway pulsed with light, symbols and numbers projected across its walls: dice, cards, probability trees, pie charts in primary colors. Its sign spun slowly in the breeze: *The Probability Pavilion: Can You Beat the Odds?*

"Last one," Leo said.

Lila touched the badges on her shirt. She hadn't counted them lately. There were several.

"Last one," she agreed. "Let's make it count."

Reciprocity: *When someone gives us something, we feel we should give something back—even when we don't have to. Be grateful, but ask: Do I really want to give?*

Chapter Ten

The Probability Pavilion

Probability

The Probability Pavilion was different from everything else in the midway. The outside was covered in projected numbers and symbols that shifted and changed—a die showing four, then two, then six. A spinning coin, heads, tails, heads. A pie chart dividing and redividing itself. It looked like a math problem had swallowed a carnival tent and was now showing everyone what it was like inside.

Lila stared at it. "It's doing a lot."

"It's showing probability in action," Leo said. He stepped closer, following one of the projected coins with his eyes. "Every time it flips, the odds of the next flip are exactly the same as before. Fifty-fifty. It doesn't matter that it was heads four times in a row."

"Right," Lila said. "I knew that."

"Did you?"

"I knew it a little."

Professor Ponder was inside, which they could see because the tent flap was open, and he was standing in the middle of the space with his arms spread wide and his purple suit somehow looking even more purple in the colored lights. He looked like the inside of a star.

"My final adventurers!" he boomed as they entered. "The last challenge. The Probability Pavilion—where we learn to understand odds, calculate chances, and make smarter decisions by knowing what's actually likely."

The interior was laid out with different stations around the edges, each one a different probability game. A spinning wheel with unequal sections. A card game with the deck showing. A set of three cups with one coin underneath. A board showing weather forecasts and actual outcomes. Each one, Leo noticed, was designed to teach a specific thing about how probability worked—and how our instincts about it often led us wrong.

A carnival worker at the center station waved them over. "Classic game first! Three cups, one golden marble. Pick the right cup and win—plus a significant step toward that badge."

Three identical red cups sat on the table, upside down. Somewhere under one of them, theoretically, was a golden marble.

Lila looked at the cups. "Okay. One in three. I've got a thirty-three percent chance."

"Exactly right," the worker said, with a look of mild surprise. "Go for it."

Lila picked the middle cup. *Empty?* She thought to herself, but trusted her gut feeling, and stuck with her choice.

The worker lifted the cup on the left. Also empty. "I'll show you one that isn't it," she said. "Now—do you want to switch to the other cup, or stay?"

Lila frowned. "It's fifty-fifty now, right? Two cups, one marble."

"Is it?" Leo said.

"There are two cups and one marble. That's fifty-fifty."

Leo was quiet for a moment. He was thinking about something.

"Actually," he said slowly, "I think it's not fifty-fifty. I think you should switch."

"What? That makes no sense. It's—"

"Think about it this way," Leo said. "When you first picked, there was a one-in-three chance you were right. That means there was a two-in-three chance the marble was in one of the other two cups. When the worker revealed one empty cup, that two-in-three chance didn't disappear—it all moved to the remaining cup. So switching gives you a two-in-three chance."

Lila stared at him. Then at the cups. Then at him again.

"That cannot be right," she said.

"It's called the Monty Hall problem," Leo said. "It's famous for being the opposite of what your instincts say."

The worker nodded. "He's right."

"Switch," Leo said.

Lila switched to the right cup. The worker lifted it.

The golden marble sat there, gleaming.

Lila made a sound that was somewhere between a gasp and a laugh. "I don't understand that," she said. "I will never understand that."

"You don't have to understand *exactly* why," Professor Ponder said, materializing at the edge of the station. "You just have to know that it's true, so that when you're faced with a choice like that, you can use the right information instead of trusting the feeling."

"The gut feeling says stay," Lila said. "Clearly."

"Your gut almost always says stay. And the math almost always says switch. Probability is full of cases like this—where what seems obvious is wrong, and what seems counterintuitive is right."

Leo had moved to a different station while this was happening. He was studying the weather board, which showed historical forecasts and how often they were right. He pointed to a section that said 70% chance of rain.

"If it says seventy percent chance of rain," he called across the tent, "that means it's definitely going to rain, right?"

"What would you say?" Professor Ponder called back.

"I'd say it means that in situations exactly like this one—same clouds, same pressure, same everything—it rains seven out of ten times. But three out of ten times, it doesn't. So no, it's not *definitely* raining. It's probably raining."

"And if you don't bring an umbrella and it doesn't rain?"

"I made a reasonable decision and got unlucky. That's different from making a bad decision."

"Yes!" Professor Ponder crossed the tent in three large strides. "This is one of the most important distinctions in probability, and in life. A good decision with a bad outcome is still a good decision. A bad decision that happens to work out is still a bad decision. We judge decisions by the process, not just the result."

Lila held up the golden marble. It was heavier than expected. "So I made a good decision by switching, even if the marble had been under the cup I switched away from."

"Exactly right."

"But it worked out."

"This time. Over many tries, switching wins two-thirds of the time. In the long run, the good decision produces better results. In any single instance, you can still be unlucky."

They worked through two more stations—the spinning wheel, where Leo calculated that certain sections came up three times as often as others and bet accordingly; and the card game, where Lila learned that tracking what cards had already been played changed the odds of what would come next.

The lesson underneath all of it, Leo thought, was the same as the jellybean jar in the Anchoring Arcade: numbers matter, and the right numbers are usually different from the first ones your gut offers.

And then the lights in the pavilion changed.

All the projected symbols—the dice, the coins, the charts—slowly faded, replaced by a warm golden glow that spread from the center of the tent outward. The pipe organ somewhere in the midway shifted to a different tune, something sweeter and more ceremonial.

Professor Ponder stood before them with the expression of someone who has watched many adventures conclude and still finds each one moving.

"My marvelous, magnificent twins," he said. "You have done something that very few visitors to this midway manage to do. You've spun the Wheel of Wants and discovered that value isn't always obvious. You've beaten the Anchoring Arcade by finding your own starting point. You've resisted temptation in the Marshmallow Maze. You've looked past the frame to the facts in the Funhouse. You've faced loss in the Labyrinth and kept going anyway. You've led instead of followed at the Carousel. You've simplified and chosen in the Paradox tent. You've known when to stop in the Swamp. You've taken a free gift without feeling obligated in return. And now you've understood that odds are real and instincts can lie."

He reached into his jacket—the same jacket from which he had produced jellybeans and tickets and various other inexplicable things all week—and removed two badges. These were different from the others. Where the others had been glittery and fun, these were solid and weighty, with a star at the center and fine engraving around the edge that read: *Decision-Maker*.

He pinned one on each of them.

"Official," he said. "Certified. Earned."

Lila looked down at hers. She touched it with one finger, very gently.

"This isn't just sparkly," she said, surprised.

"No. It's not." Professor Ponder smiled. "It means you've learned to ask the questions. *What's my anchor? Is it worth the wait? What's the real deal? What could I gain? Am I following or leading? What do I really want? Is it still worth it? Do I really want to give? What are my chances?* Carry those questions with you, and they'll serve you better than any sparkly thing."

Leo adjusted his glasses. "You'll be back next year?"

"Every year, new challenges. Because the world is full of decisions, and there are always new ways to study them." Professor Ponder tipped his hat—the impossible, wobbling hat that had somehow stayed on his head through this entire week. "Now go home. Rest. Eat something non-carnival-related. And the next time you face a choice that feels hard or confusing, ask yourself which question applies."

As they walked out of the Probability Pavilion and back onto the midway, the evening was coming in fast, turning the lights of the carnival gold and orange against a darkening sky. Rides sparkled. The calliope played. Somewhere near the exit, Mrs. Higginbottom's cat probably wasn't stuck in a tree, and nothing exciting was happening in Ashwood Bluff.

But Lila and Leo were different.

Not in a way anyone could see, exactly—they still looked like the same twins who'd charged through the golden archway at the beginning of the week, one of them leading, one of them thinking. But inside, something had shifted. They'd been shown that their own brains could trick them—and they'd learned the questions to ask when that happened.

Lila nudged Leo with her shoulder. "Think we can outsmart him next year?"

"Odds are yes," Leo said. "But we should probably do the reading first."

"There's reading?"

"There's always reading."

Lila groaned—but she was smiling.

They walked home through the Ashwood Bluff streets as the carnival lights faded behind them, badges pinned to their shirts, heads full of questions, and at least one of them already planning which books to check out from the library before next summer.

The other one was still thinking about the marshmallows.

Probability: *Understanding how likely something is to happen helps us make smarter decisions. Good decisions are about process, not just outcomes—ask: What are my chances?*

The End.

The Decision-Maker's Toolkit

Keep this page handy. The next time you face a tough choice, run through these nine questions. You don't have to use them all—just the ones that fit the moment.

1. What's my anchor?

Anchoring

The first number or idea you hear can pull your thinking toward it. Ask whether your starting point is trustworthy—or whether you should ignore it and think fresh.

2. Is it worth the wait?

Delayed Gratification

Most things worth having require patience. Before grabbing the small reward in front of you, ask if a bigger one is coming.

3. What's the real deal?

Framing

The way something is described isn't always the way it actually is. Strip away the exciting words or the scary words and look for the plain fact underneath.

4. What could I gain?

Loss Aversion

Don't let the fear of losing what you have stop you from going after something better. The thing you already own isn't always worth keeping.

5. Am I following or leading?

Herd Mentality

Just because everyone else is doing it doesn't mean it's right for you. Ask whether you actually want this—or whether you're just going along.

6. What do I really want?

Paradox of Choice

When too many options make your brain freeze, narrow it down by knowing yourself. Pick what you love. The rest doesn't matter.

7. Is it still worth it?

Sunk Cost Fallacy

What you've already spent is gone whether you continue or not. Decide based on what's ahead, not what's behind.

8. Do I really want to give?

Reciprocity

When someone gives you something, you'll feel pulled to give back. That feeling is real—but you still get to choose. Be grateful without being trapped.

9. What are my chances?

Probability

Knowing the odds doesn't guarantee outcomes—but it makes you a smarter chooser. Good decisions are about process, not luck.

The midway is always open. Choose wisely.

A Look Ahead

Book Two: The Persuasion Bazaar

A year went by.

Lila and Leo did the things twelve-year-olds do when they are quietly becoming thirteen. They went to school. They argued about whose turn it was to walk the dog. They each, in their own way, used the toolkit Professor Ponder had given them — though they would not have called it that. Lila stopped reaching for the first bright thing in the store. Leo started, occasionally, taking the chance. Their decision-maker badges hung above their desks, slightly dusty, and the questions Professor Ponder had taught them had settled somewhere behind their eyes, where useful things go to wait.

The carnival did not return.

Lila checked. She checked the empty fairgrounds at the edge of Ashwood Bluff in early June, and again in late June, and again at the beginning of July, by which point Leo had begun to give her looks. There were no rides. There were no lanterns. There was a perfectly ordinary field with perfectly ordinary woods and a perfectly ordinary cat — Whiskers, naturally — sleeping on the perfectly ordinary fence.

"He's not coming back," Leo said.

"He might."

"He's not."

He wasn't.

But something else was.

On the second Saturday of August, Lila woke at sunrise to a smell she could not place — yeast and cinnamon and something roasted and dark, threaded through with something sweet. She got out of bed. She went to the window. And the town square, which the night before had been a perfectly ordinary empty square, was now not empty at all.

It was full of canopies.

It was full of carts.

It was full of people who had not been there the night before, arranging displays of things she could not entirely make out from her window, while somewhere in the middle of it all a sign — gold-lettered, slightly wobbly, exactly the right shade of purple — announced that *Professor Ponder's Magnificent Market* was open for business.

The lessons of the carnival had been about choosing.

The lessons of the market, she would soon discover, were about something else entirely. They were about the people who wanted her to choose a particular way, and the small, invisible levers they pulled to make her want it too. They were about pitches, and pressure, and the gentle art of being convinced.

They were about persuasion.

And this time, the twins had a budget.

...

Professor Ponder's Magnificent Market: The Persuasion Bazaar

Book Two of Professor Ponder's Academy of Magnificent Mistakes

Available now

About the Author

Zachary Urban is an affordable housing policy professional, civic leader, and writer based in Denver, Colorado. He holds a degree in Communications from Colorado State University and has spent over two decades working at the intersection of government, community development, and public service. He is a columnist for the Neighborhood Gazette, a local publication serving the Wheat Ridge, Colorado community.

A longtime student of behavioral economics, Zach became convinced that the field's most powerful ideas—anchoring, loss aversion, the sunk cost fallacy, the pull of the crowd—were too important to leave to adults alone. His conviction was sharpened at home, where his two children illustrated the lessons every day. His daughter, a fastidious saver and a serious, studious student, weighs every decision before making it. His son loves games, gambling, and the rush of taking a chance. Two siblings, two completely different decision-making styles, both navigating the same confusing world.

He wrote The Choice Carnival to give his son tools for thinking through risk, to give his daughter permission to take the right kind of chances, and to give every young reader a vocabulary for the invisible forces that shape their choices. The twins Lila and Leo are loosely modeled on his own kids—though, he is quick to note, his real children are even more interesting.

This is his first children's book.

Acknowledgements

To Melinda, who heard every draft, every doubt, and every half-formed idea at the kitchen table, and who always said the right thing — which was usually "keep going."

To Isabella and Isaiah, who are nothing like Lila and Leo, except in the ways that matter most. Thank you for letting me borrow pieces of who you are. The book is yours.

To the early readers — kids and grown-ups both — who told me which parts made them laugh, which parts they didn't understand, and which parts they wanted to read twice. You are the reason any of this is any good.

To the teachers, librarians, and parents who pick up books like this one and put them in the hands of children: there is no more important work.

And to the reader who has come this far: thank you. Carry the questions with you. They'll serve you well.

— Z.U.

www.ingramcontent.com/pod-product-compliance
Lightning Source LLC
LaVergne TN
LVHW040516210926
848480LV00005BA/1480
* 9 7 9 8 2 3 4 0 9 0 9 2 8 *